DATE DUE
Fecha Para Retornar

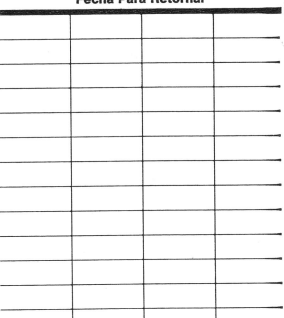

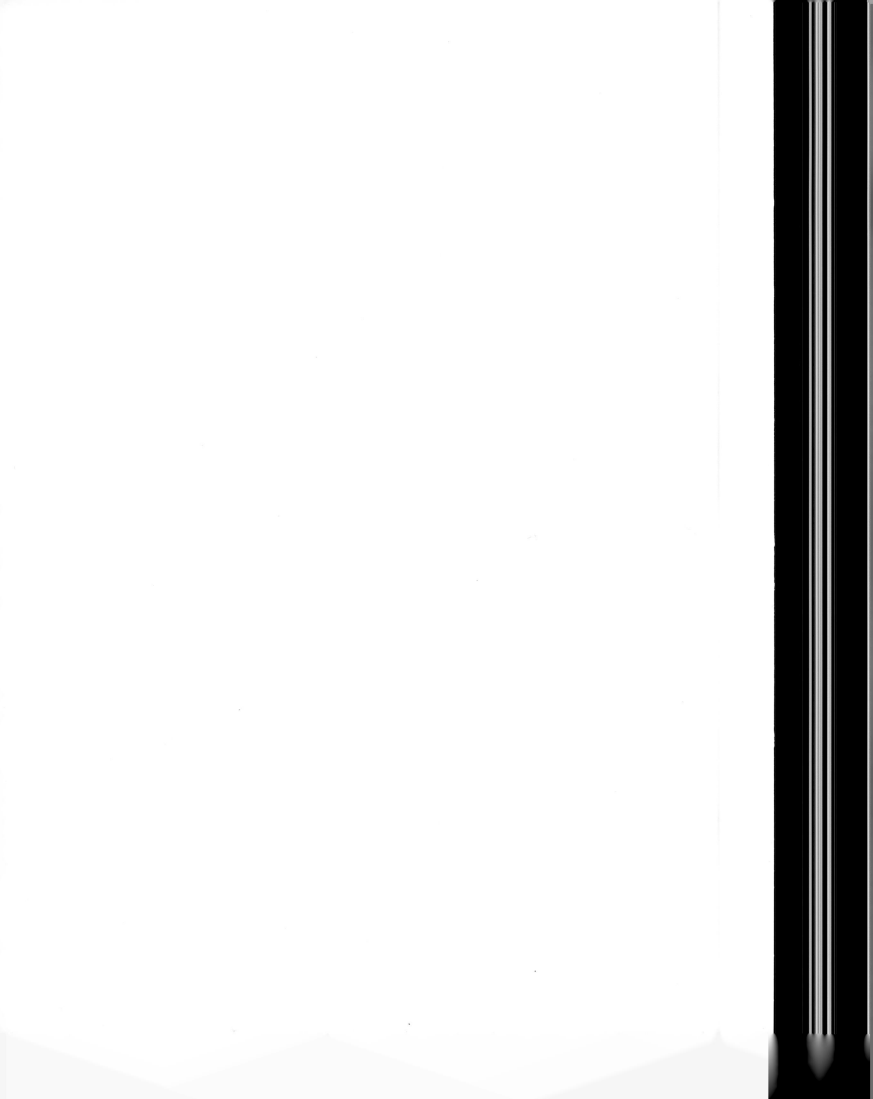

SAVING OUR WORLD

NEW ENERGY SOURCES

Nigel Hawkes

COPPER BEECH BOOKS

BROOKFIELD • CONNECTICUT

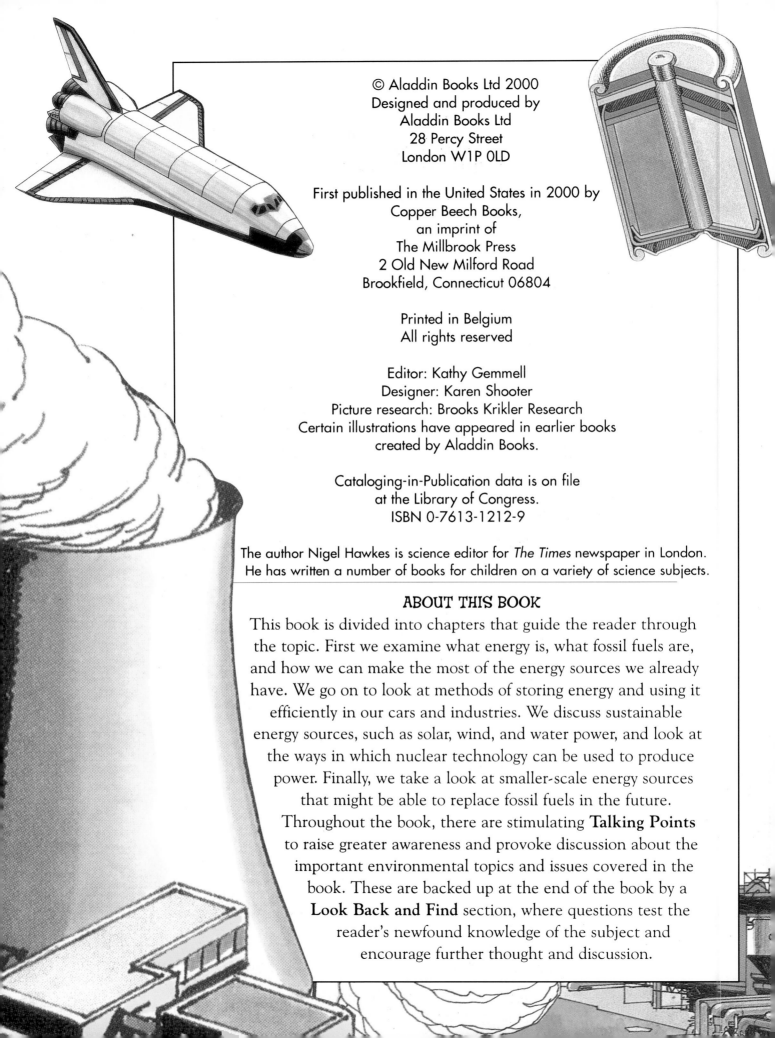

© Aladdin Books Ltd 2000
Designed and produced by
Aladdin Books Ltd
28 Percy Street
London W1P 0LD

First published in the United States in 2000 by
Copper Beech Books,
an imprint of
The Millbrook Press
2 Old New Milford Road
Brookfield, Connecticut 06804

Printed in Belgium
All rights reserved

Editor: Kathy Gemmell
Designer: Karen Shooter
Picture research: Brooks Krikler Research
Certain illustrations have appeared in earlier books
created by Aladdin Books.

Cataloging-in-Publication data is on file
at the Library of Congress.
ISBN 0-7613-1212-9

The author Nigel Hawkes is science editor for *The Times* newspaper in London. He has written a number of books for children on a variety of science subjects.

ABOUT THIS BOOK

This book is divided into chapters that guide the reader through the topic. First we examine what energy is, what fossil fuels are, and how we can make the most of the energy sources we already have. We go on to look at methods of storing energy and using it efficiently in our cars and industries. We discuss sustainable energy sources, such as solar, wind, and water power, and look at the ways in which nuclear technology can be used to produce power. Finally, we take a look at smaller-scale energy sources that might be able to replace fossil fuels in the future. Throughout the book, there are stimulating **Talking Points** to raise greater awareness and provoke discussion about the important environmental topics and issues covered in the book. These are backed up at the end of the book by a **Look Back and Find** section, where questions test the reader's newfound knowledge of the subject and encourage further thought and discussion.

CONTENTS

p. 4-5 New Energy Now!

Why do we need new energy sources?

CHAPTER 1: WHAT IS ENERGY?

p. 6-7 Where energy comes from

How does energy work? What are fossil fuels?

p. 8-9 Making the most of it

What can we do to save energy?

CHAPTER 2: BEING MORE EFFICIENT

p. 10-11 Storing electricity

How do batteries work?
Can batteries power electric cars?

p. 12-13 Hydrogen and fuel cells

What are fuel cells and how can
they help to ease the energy crisis?

CHAPTER 3: ALTERNATIVES IN ACTION

p. 14-15 Solar power

What can be driven by solar power?

p. 16-17 Water power

What is hydroelectricity?
How do we get energy from the tides?

p. 18-19 Wind power

Where can wind farms be built?

p. 20-21 Biomass

What is biomass?
Find out how plants can be used to fuel cars.

p. 22-23 Nuclear fission

What happens in a nuclear power station? Is nuclear
power a solution to disappearing energy sources?

CHAPTER 4: THE WAY FORWARD?

p. 24-25 Nuclear fusion

What is fusion? How might it
affect our ability to produce energy?

p. 26-27 Longshots

What other ideas are there for producing
clean, efficient, and sustainable energy?

p. 28-29 Look Back and Find

Test yourself to see how much you know
about new energy sources.

p. 30 You Be Environmental!

Learn how you can help to slow the energy crisis.

p. 31 GLOSSARY

p. 32 INDEX

New Energy Now!

Why do we need it?

Once, all our energy came from the sun or from fire. Today, we use far more energy, from many different sources, than we have ever used in the past. Continuing to provide this energy is a huge challenge because the main sources we rely on — oil, gas, and coal (below) — will all eventually run out.

We need new energy sources that are renewed as they are used. As the world's population increases and more and more people expect the standards of living enjoyed in rich, developed countries, the demand for energy will grow very fast. We do not have much time to develop the new sources of energy we desperately need.

Energy from the sun is used to run the biggest solar power station in California (above) and specially designed solar-powered cars (right).

Which way now?

There is a second reason we need new energy sources. Burning carbon-based fuels such as coal, oil, and gas pollutes the air (left). Although much can be done to reduce the damage, the scale of human activity is now so great that the pollution is beginning to affect the earth's climate. Carbon dioxide, the gas created by burning carbon-based fuels, is building up in the atmosphere and gradually making the earth warmer. So far, this global warming has been slight, but without more nonpolluting sources of energy it will worsen much faster. Some way must be found to feed our need for energy without doing permanent damage to the world in which we live. Developing new, clean, sustainable sources of energy is the only way to do that.

CHAPTER ONE

What is Energy?

Where energy comes from

Energy is what makes things work. It cannot be created from nothing and it cannot be destroyed. All that happens is that one form of energy is converted into another. Almost all the energy we use comes from the sun. Sunlight makes plants grow, and plants provide us with food and fuel. The sun also creates the weather.

► Plants and the sun

Plants use sunlight to make carbohydrates in their leaves. They need carbohydrates, plus water and light, to be able to grow. Plants also produce the oxygen we breathe.

Carbohydrates

Food energy

The energy that we, and other animals, need to survive comes from food. Plants provide us with much of this food fuel. As we digest food, it releases its energy, which is used by our muscles when we move. Fats and sugars store most energy. Today, many people lead inactive lives and eat more than they need. Others cannot grow enough food to provide the energy they need to survive.

Energy from trees

Trees are among the best stores of solar energy (energy from the sun) because wood can be used as fuel. When early humans discovered fire, wood was the fuel they used. Today, it remains an important source of energy for millions of people.

Fossil fuels

Coal, oil, and gas are the remains of long-dead animals or plants that sunlight helped to grow millions of years ago. These plants and animals gradually decayed (broke down) into the ground to form a store of fossilized solar energy in the earth's crust. This is why coal, oil, and gas are known as fossil fuels. We mine for coal and drill for oil and gas to use their energy to provide heat and power.

Coal

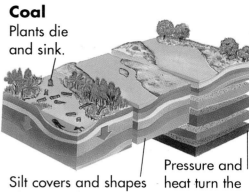

Plants die and sink.

Silt covers and shapes plants into hard layers.

Pressure and heat turn the layers into coal.

Oil and gas

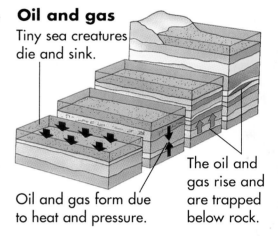

Tiny sea creatures die and sink.

Oil and gas form due to heat and pressure.

The oil and gas rise and are trapped below rock.

▶ Sun, wind, and water

The sun's heat controls the weather. It evaporates water from the oceans to form clouds from which rain falls. It also creates winds, which sweep across the oceans and generate waves. Running water, wind, and waves are all forms of stored solar energy. By concentrating these stores, we can make use of the energy they provide.

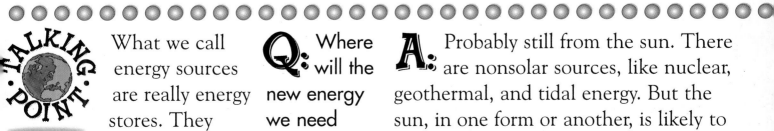

TALKING POINT

What we call energy sources are really energy stores. They store energy from the sun.

Q: Where will the new energy we need come from?

A: Probably still from the sun. There are nonsolar sources, like nuclear, geothermal, and tidal energy. But the sun, in one form or another, is likely to provide most of our future energy.

Making the most of it

Using less energy is the best way to reduce pollution, extend the life of existing fuel resources, and save the planet from global warming. Energy conservation, as this is called, could be the most important "source" of energy this century.

▲ Diesel fuel in cars

Cars running on diesel do more miles to the gallon than gasoline engines, which makes oil reserves last longer. But there are worries about the health effects of diesel exhaust.

▼ Recycled car

A lot of energy is needed to make the steel, plastic, rubber, and other materials that cars contain. Although steel can be recycled at scrap yards, new designs that make it easier to separate out the other materials for reuse are needed. This BMW design is made from recycled (blue) and recyclable (green) materials.

Energy consumption

20 percent of the world's population consumes 60 percent of the world's total energy supply. This chart shows roughly how much energy is used, per person, in different parts of the world.

(Bar chart: Tons of fuel used per person per year, y-axis 0–7, categories A–J)

KEY
A: USA / Canada
B: Japan / Australia / New Zealand
C: Western Europe
D: Commonwealth of Independent States / Eastern Europe / Iran
E: Middle East
F: Latin America
G: China
H: Other Asia / Turkey
I: Africa
J: India

◄ Tire recycling

Tires are very difficult to recycle. Getting back the original rubber from worn-out tires has been compared to "unbaking" a cake to extract the ingredients. Old tires can be chopped up and added to road surfaces, but this is a waste of a potentially valuable material.

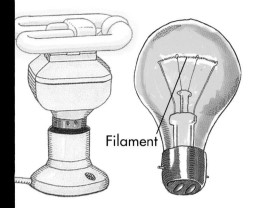

Filament

◀ Energy-saving bulbs

Traditional light bulbs (left) use a glowing filament to create light, but in the process they also create heat. Energy-saving fluorescent bulbs (far left) operate at near room temperature, create no waste heat, use only a fifth as much energy to create the same light, and last much longer. But they are much more expensive to buy, so they are used mainly for lamps that stay on a lot.

▶ Energy-saving appliances

Refrigerators, washing machines, and dishwashers can vary enormously in the amount of energy they use, depending on how well they have been designed. An efficient machine can use less than half the energy used by an inefficient one.

The A on this refrigerator label shows that it is energy-efficient.

▼ Going green

Using household goods made from recycled paper means fewer trees need to be chopped down to make the paper. This saves wood, one of our most precious resources.

TALKING POINT

In theory, energy conservation looks like a good idea. But energy use continues to go up and few people try very hard to save it.

Q: Why isn't energy conservation more successful?

A: When energy is cheap, it costs more to save it than to use it, so many people don't bother. Some people choose to have a warmer house or get a bigger car, rather than a more energy efficient one.

CHAPTER TWO

Being More Efficient

Storing electricity

Electricity is one of the most convenient forms of energy, vital for lighting, heating, and household appliances. But electricity is expensive to store, especially in large amounts. Almost all of it has to be generated at the same time as it is being used. This means that power stations have to be turned on and off to meet changing demand.

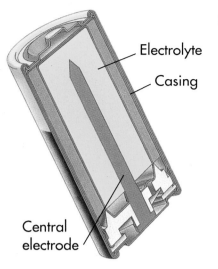

Electrolyte

Casing

Central electrode

▲ How batteries work

Batteries are good at storing small amounts of electricity. They turn chemical energy into electrical energy using a chemical called an electrolyte, which is acid in a car battery or ammonium chloride in a "dry" cell (above). When a circuit between the zinc casing of the cell and the central electrode is completed, a chemical reaction between the electrolyte and the casing creates an electric current. But making a battery takes fifty times as much energy as it ever produces.

◄ Electric bus

The lack of good batteries has held back the electric car. Even the best will only last for about 120 miles before having to be recharged. This is too short a distance for most private cars but is fine for some urban buses. However, batteries are expensive and can be recharged only so often before they fail.

◄ Recharging

In the past, electric cars had to be recharged slowly overnight. But new technology has made it possible to recharge ordinary lead-acid batteries in the same time that it takes to fill the tank of the average car. This means that recharging stations like this one in Los Angeles may one day replace today's gas stations.

◄ Hybrid car

A hybrid car uses batteries and a small engine to recharge the batteries. When full performance is not required — in traffic, for example — the engine generates electricity to drive the car and keep the batteries charged. Hybrid cars can go farther than pure electric cars, and have lean-burn gasoline engines that consume less fuel than ordinary cars.

The water in the top reservoir represents stored electricity.

Water is pumped through tunnels in the rock.

▲ Storage station

Large amounts of electricity can be stored in pumped storage plants like the Dinorwic hydroelectric project in Wales. Electricity generated at night is used to pump water to a great height. As demand picks up the next day, the water is released to generate electricity.

TALKING POINT

In the developed world, people take batteries for granted. But in some parts of the world they simply cost too much for people to afford. Many people cannot even run a transistor radio.

Q: So how do we make cheaper, better batteries?

A: Batteries might not be the answer. British inventor Trevor Baylis went back to an older idea — clockwork — to provide cheap radios for poor countries. A single winding of the clockwork radio takes hardly any time and provides half an hour's listening.

Hydrogen and fuel cells

The best way to store electricity may be in the form of hydrogen, a gas that can be produced by passing electricity through water. It can be used as fuel in ordinary engines or in fuel cells, which are devices that convert hydrogen back into electricity. Hydrogen produces no pollution: the only "exhaust" is clean water.

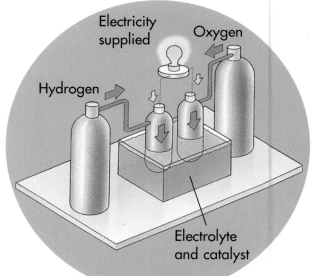

◄ Space shuttle

All manned spacecraft since the Apollo moon missions of the 1960s have used fuel cells to generate their electricity and produce their drinking water. They are reliable and effective, but have until recently been considered much too expensive for use on the earth.

◄ Fuel cells

Although they have long been known to work, fuel cells are just beginning to become practical for day-to-day electricity production. New components have greatly increased their efficiency. These fuel cells are used to power the van shown at the top of page 13.

Huge fuel cells (below) are used as power stations, generating up to 200 kilowatts of electricity — enough for 150 homes.

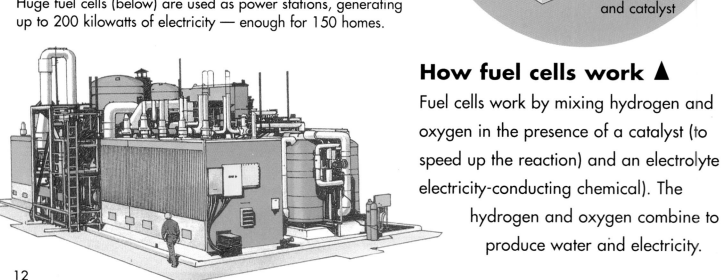

How fuel cells work ▲

Fuel cells work by mixing hydrogen and oxygen in the presence of a catalyst (to speed up the reaction) and an electrolyte (an electricity-conducting chemical). The hydrogen and oxygen combine to produce water and electricity.

▼ Hydrogen-powered car

Hydrogen can be burned in a normal engine, replacing gasoline. The result is a much cleaner exhaust, with no carbon monoxide or dioxide. But hydrogen is highly flammable (catches fire easily), and the methods for producing, storing, and filling up with it need to be perfected before the hydrogen car can become a practical reality.

Fuel cells are kept in here.

Zero emissions ▲

Because fuel cells produce no emissions (exhaust) apart from water, they are a very clean fuel option for vehicles. This van, used by the City of Westminster Council in London, is powered by zero-emission fuel cells.

Fuel-cell car ▼

German carmaker Daimler-Benz has made four fuel-cell vehicles. The New Electric Car (NECAR) IV, launched in 1999 as a demonstration of the technology, is powered by a fuel cell small enough to fit into an average engine compartment or under the floor.

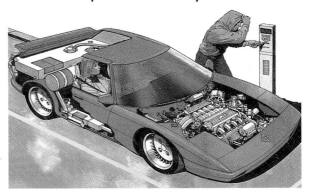

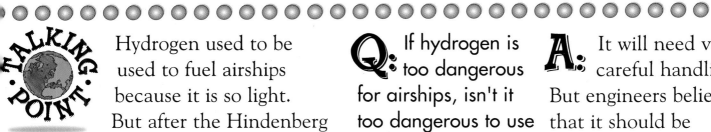

TALKING POINT

Hydrogen used to be used to fuel airships because it is so light. But after the Hindenberg airship burst into flames in New Jersey in 1937, helium was used.

Q: If hydrogen is too dangerous for airships, isn't it too dangerous to use as a fuel for cars?

A: It will need very careful handling. But engineers believe that it should be possible to store and distribute safely.

CHAPTER THREE

Alternatives in Action

Solar power

Energy from the sun is plentiful and free, but it is thinly spread. This means that to capture worthwhile amounts of it, large, expensive collectors are needed. Trees have leaves, with an enormous collective surface area, to do the job. The human version of leaves are solar collectors. These use the sun's heat to warm water or operate solar cells, which convert sunshine directly into electricity.

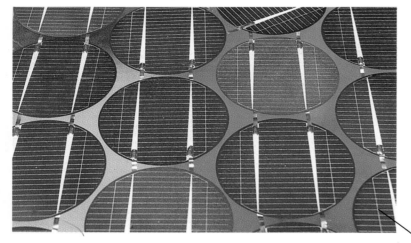

▲ Solar cells

When light is absorbed by a solar cell, tiny particles called electrons are released. They move, creating a current. Cells are usually made of silicon — the material that computer chips are made of. The best solar cell, made by U.S. engineers, can convert nearly a third of the sunlight falling on it into electricity. It uses lenses or mirrors to concentrate the sunlight nearly fiftyfold. Solar cells can be linked together in arrays (panels) pointing at the sun to create a solar power station.

Solar cell

► Solar furnace

Solar furnaces like this one at Odeillo in France work by focusing sunlight onto a single spot. They use the curved side of a large building as a reflector, and the concentrated sunlight creates temperatures high enough to melt a steel armor plating. Other kinds of solar power stations use mirrors that track the passage of the sun across the sky.

Curved mirrors reflect light onto a central tower.

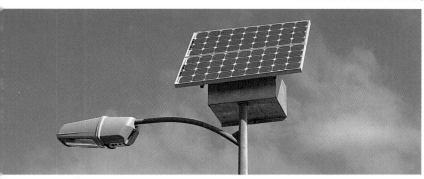

▲ Solar-powered streetlight

Solar power can be used to produce electricity on a very small scale. In sunny areas, one collector panel can collect and store enough power during daylight hours to run a streetlight when it gets dark.

Solar cells

Solar plane

Solar cells on the surface of the wings and tail of a light aircraft can create enough electricity to drive a propeller and keep the plane in the air — as long as the sun is shining. Many designs of solar-powered cars have also been developed.

Propeller

Solar cells

◄ Solar-powered hotel

In the Himalayas in Nepal, where there is a lot of sun and little or no pollution to block its rays, this hotel can be run on solar power alone. In Colorado, a man has set up solar installations that generate enough electricity not only to power his home but also to sell to the local power company.

TALKING POINT The sun produces lots of energy, but we are limited in how much of it we can use. In the north, where energy demand is greatest in winter, the sun doesn't shine for long each day.

Q: What happens to solar power at night, or when it is cloudy?

A: Solar energy doesn't operate at night and is greatly reduced by clouds. The long-term solution is to find better ways of storing it.

Water power

Rivers and streams have been used to drive water wheels for more than a thousand years. But water power is still one of the best sources of energy. The world's biggest power stations are driven by turbines turned by the power of water.

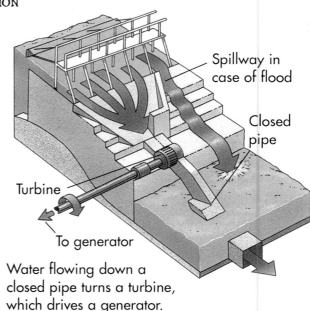

Spillway in case of flood

Closed pipe

Turbine

To generator

Water flowing down a closed pipe turns a turbine, which drives a generator.

▼ Hydroelectric dams

Hydroelectric schemes use huge dams to block the flow of rivers and create enormous lakes. The water is allowed to escape down tunnels to drive turbines that generate electricity. The fuel — water — is free, but building the dam is usually very expensive and large areas of land have to be flooded to create the lake in which to store the water. Thousands of people have to be moved from their homes and large areas of farmland are destroyed.

▲ How turbines work

Turbines are like fans, or propellers, that are turned by the water flowing over them. The farther the water has to fall from the dam to the turbines, the more power it produces. Hydroelectric projects use many turbines and can produce enormous amounts of electricity.

Creating electricity

The Itaipu Dam in Brazil is one of the biggest hydroelectric projects in the world. It was designed to produce over 13,000 megawatts of electricity.

Small-scale hydro projects

Local hydroelectric projects built on a stream can provide enough electricity for a whole village, without needing to build a dam and flood farmland. This one in Yunan, China, provides power for a farming commune. China is planning to build 1,000 similar small-scale hydroelectric projects a year. Worldwide, the number of projects is expected to almost double by 2010.

Turbines are kept in here.

Generators

Turbine blades

▲ Tidal power

In places where there are high tides, water can be trapped by movable gates, then channeled through turbines as the tide falls. The tidal plant at La Rance in France has operated well for many years. Building costs for tidal plants are high, but they have a very long life.

TALKING POINT The energy produced by water power is free, created by the sun's heat, which evaporates water so that it later falls as rain to fill the reservoirs. It is also renewable.

Q: So why aren't many more hydro projects being set up?

A: Costs are high because of the huge size of the dams that are needed. And the environment suffers by being flooded, which ruins valuable farmland.

Wind power

The first windmills appeared about 1,400 years ago in Asia, and in the nineteenth century millions were built in the United States. Now wind power is making a comeback, in the form of large wind turbines with blades like those on an aircraft propeller. Big improvements have been made in the past fifteen years, reducing costs and increasing reliability.

▲ Modern sails

Some modern cargo ships reduce fuel costs by using the wind to blow large rectangular sails. The sails are mechanically operated so they do not need large crews to work them as they did on the old sailing ships.

▲ Offshore wind

Shallow water offshore is a good place to put turbines, as the wind there is often strong. At Onsveig wind farm in Denmark, there are eleven turbines, each able to produce 450 kilowatts. In a year, the farm produces enough electricity to power 4,500 homes. It generates 50 percent more power than an onshore farm, but it cost twice as much to build.

► Wind farms

Places with strong and steady winds for much of the year are ideal as wind farm sites. Building large collections of turbines grouped together not only makes the most of windy places, but also spreads the cost of the power lines needed to carry the electricity away.

The blades spin fastest if they are facing straight into the wind.

Blade

Generator

Gears

Gearing up the wind

The wind turns the blades quite slowly, so a gearbox is needed to increase the speed to 1,500 rpm (revolutions per minute). This generates electricity of the right frequency to feed into the grid (national electricity system).

Blade

Types of wind power ▼

Most wind turbines have a horizontal axis that carries a two- or three-bladed rotor. But the rotors have to be turned to face the wind if the wind direction changes. So designs with a vertical axis, such as the Darrieus windmill (3), and designs with two vertical blades that swivel as the wind increases (2), may prove to be more efficient in the long run. Both are in development.

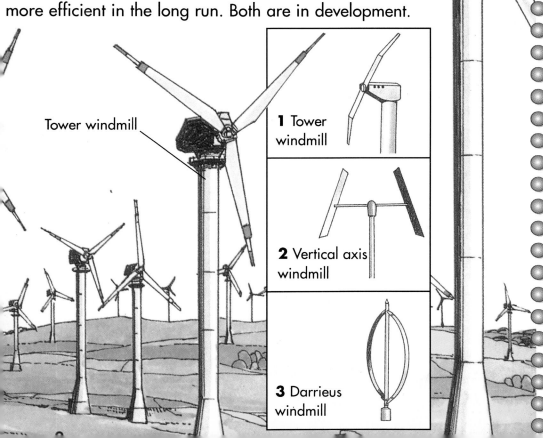

Tower windmill

1 Tower windmill

2 Vertical axis windmill

3 Darrieus windmill

TALKING POINT

Wind turbines produce clean, renewable power, but some people are opposed to them.

Q: What are the drawbacks of wind turbines, and why aren't more being built?

A: The windiest places are usually remote and often beautiful. Protesters say that these areas should not be spoiled by having hundreds of machines planted on them. In countries with a lot of space, such as the United States, this is not generally a problem, but in small, crowded countries like Britain, planning permission is often refused. Building offshore helps, but is twice as expensive.

Biomass

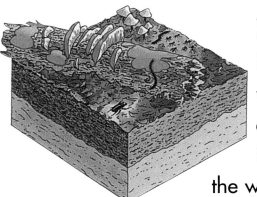

Biomass is the material produced by growing plants, which every year store about ten times as much energy as the human population uses. Wood is the most important plant store, providing about 15 percent of the world's energy. Some crops can be turned into fuel. Domestic trash is also classed as biomass, as much of it is made from plant products.

▶ Biomass energy

In the United States, wood and wood wastes account for most biomass energy, followed by domestic waste, which is burnt in huge incinerators to produce heat, then gases from landfill sites and agricultral waste.

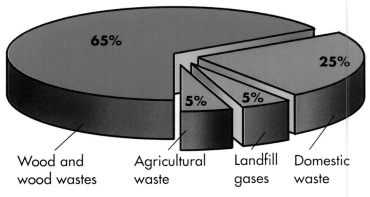

65%

25%

5%   5%

Wood and wood wastes   Agricultural waste   Landfill gases   Domestic waste

◀ Sugarcane fuel

Sugarcane produces large plants that are milled to extract the sugar. The cane can be fermented to produce ethanol — the kind of alcohol found in beer — which can be used as a substitute for gasoline.

▶ Alcohol car

Brazil has pioneered techniques for using the alcohol produced by fermenting plants as fuel. The alcohol can either be used by itself or blended with gasoline. It is dispensed to cars from normal gas stations.

Waste landfills

When garbage is dumped on a landfill site, it decays to produce methane (natural gas). In the past, this gas was wasted, but today it is common to extract it using tubes driven into the decaying garbage, then use it as a fuel. In addition to providing energy, extracting the gas also reduces the risk of accidental methane explosions at the landfill site.

► Fuel from waste

Animal waste can be converted into gas in simple digesters. The waste decays inside a chamber with no air in it, producing methane gas. This can then be burned to heat homes and provide light.

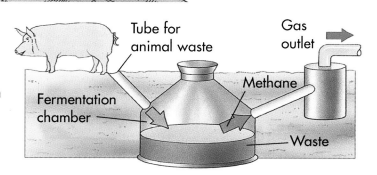

Tube for animal waste

Gas outlet

Methane

Fermentation chamber

Waste

▼ Biogas plant

A gas, such as methane, that is produced from animal or plant waste is known as a biogas. The methane given off from this small-scale biogas digester in Madras, India, can be used for cooking, and the residue makes good fertilizer for spreading over crops.

Firewood is a very important source of energy for heating and cooking in poor countries. But as populations grow, firewood is getting scarce.

Q: What can be done to maintain supplies of firewood in developing countries?

A: Replanting fast-growing timber, or using trees that provide harvests year after year could help sustain supplies.

Nuclear fission

Nuclear power is the only major source of energy that is not ultimately dependent on the sun. It involves splitting the atoms of substances called uranium and plutonium. This releases large amounts of energy that can be used to generate electricity. About 20 percent of the United States' electricity, compared to over 80 percent of France's, comes from nuclear power.

◀ Splitting the atom

Nucleus
U-235 atom

Neutron

Neutron

Neutron

Energy

Neutron

When an atom of uranium-235 is hit by a particle called a neutron, its nucleus (the center of the atom) may split. If it does, it releases a lot of energy, and at least two fresh neutrons fly off. They cause two more nuclei to split in a chain reaction. This splitting process is called fission.

1 Thin vertical tubes filled with uranium dioxide fuel are arranged so the fission chain reaction runs steadily, without getting out of control.

2 A coolant flows between the tubes to absorb heat.

3 The heat is used to produce steam in a heat exchanger.

4 The steam is then used to drive turbines linked to generators that produce electricity.

◀ Nuclear power station

Nuclear power stations use the energy of fission to generate electricity. A nuclear plant generates around 1,200 megawatts — which is more than a thousand large wind turbines generate — and works night and day. One advantage of nuclear power is that, unlike coal-fired power stations, it produces no carbon dioxide, so it can be a big help in reducing global warming.

Nuclear-powered submarine ▶

Small nuclear reactors are used to power submarines. Because they can operate underwater (unlike diesel engines) and use very little fuel, they allow submarines to remain submerged for months. The first voyage under the North Pole icecap was made by a nuclear submarine.

Nuclear reactor is kept behind a shield.

◀ Nuclear waste

The ashes left by the fission process are very dangerous and must be buried or kept isolated from people for thousands of years before they are safe. Radioactivity levels at and around nuclear plants are measured regularly.

▶ Radiation safety

Nuclear plants can go wrong. At the Chernobyl plant in the Ukraine in 1986, large amounts of poisonous and radioactive fission products (atoms produced by the splitting of uranium) leaked and spread into the air. Large areas around Chernobyl had to be cleared of people after the accident and are still uninhabited today. A new design of nuclear reactor, which has fuel in the form of a bed of "pebbles," may be safer because it shuts itself down automatically if anything starts to go wrong.

TALKING POINT

Nuclear power produces a lot of electricity without carbon dioxide emissions. Many plants work successfully around the world.

Q: So why don't environmentalists support nuclear plants, since they help reduce the carbon emissions that add to global warming?

A: Nuclear safety, long-term disposal of waste, and the danger of fuel being used for nuclear bombs worry people even more than global warming.

CHAPTER FOUR

The Way Forward?

Nuclear fusion

A second kind of nuclear reaction can also generate energy. Instead of fission, which is the splitting of a large atom, it involves combining two small atoms. This is called fusion and is the reaction that powers the sun and the stars, and that makes the hydrogen bomb a fearsome weapon.

How fusion works

Two atoms called deuterium and tritium (both forms of hydrogen) will combine if temperatures are high enough. They produce a heavier atom called helium, plus a particle called a neutron, and lots of heat. Making this happen in a controlled way is very difficult.

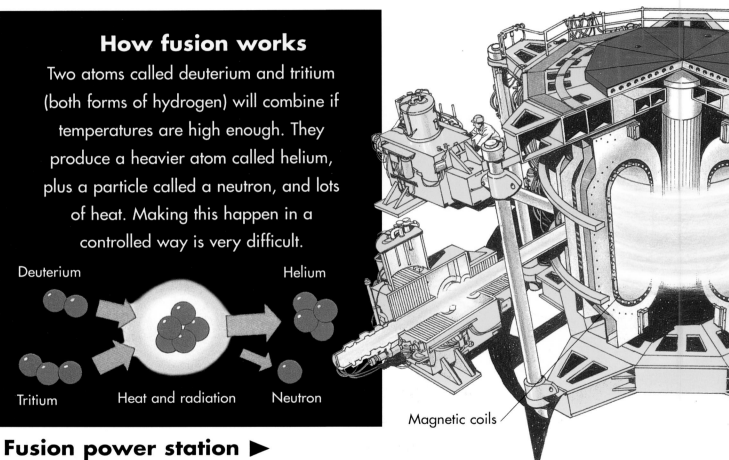

Deuterium

Helium

Tritium

Heat and radiation

Neutron

Magnetic coils

Fusion power station ▶

Nobody has yet made a fusion power station, but they know how to. The deuterium and tritium would be contained inside a donut-shaped vessel and heated to 212 million degrees Fahrenheit. As this is far too hot for any material to tolerate, the fused atoms would be prevented from touching the sides by shaped magnetic fields. The heat would be extracted to raise steam to drive generators.

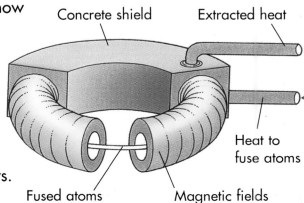

Concrete shield

Extracted heat

Heat to fuse atoms

Fused atoms

Magnetic fields

◄ H-bomb

A hydrogen bomb is a fusion reaction. The huge temperatures needed to make atoms fuse are created using an atomic (fission) bomb as a trigger. The resulting explosion is big enough to destroy a city. The largest ever tested made a bang equal to 550 million tons of the high explosive TNT.

▼ Tokamak

The best results in fusion experiments have come from machines in which the fuel is inside a pipe curled around in a complete circle (see page 24). This shape was first tried in Russia and the machines are called tokamaks, a Russian word. The Tokamak Reactor in Princeton, New Jersey, has produced short bursts of energy.

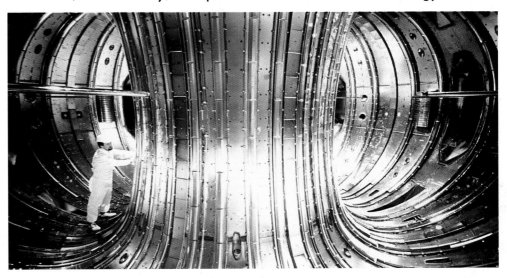

The next step in fusion

A worldwide collaboration called the International Thermonuclear Experimental Reactor (ITER) may be the way forward for fusion technology. ITER is designed to prove that fusion can be tamed and turned into a practical energy source. Europe, Russia, the United States, and Japan will all contribute to ITER, which will cost at least $10 billion.

A tokamak fusion reactor

In theory, fusion power is cleaner than fission, and fuel is everlasting. But research has been going on for fifty years, without yet producing a single watt of power.

Q: Is there any point in putting more money into fusion research?

A: There has been progress but it is slow, and fusion power would also be expensive. Perhaps the money would be better spent improving solar, water, or wind power.

Longshots

Lots of other ideas for producing energy have been tried, and some may make an important contribution in the future. But research in the past ten years has shown that most of these ideas are either impractical or too expensive. Unless there is a major breakthrough, they are unlikely to provide much energy soon.

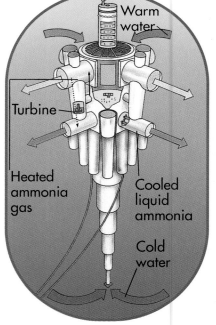

▲ Ocean thermals

Using temperature differences between deep and surface water could be a source of energy. Tests that heat liquid ammonia to a gas and then flow it over turbines have proved it possible, but costs would be high.

Geothermal plant

Using the heat of the earth is a potential goldmine. Natural hot springs already run geothermal power stations in Iceland (above), New Zealand, and California. But extracting heat from dry rock (left) by pumping down water and getting it back as steam — or at least hot water — proved tricky. The machinery became clogged with dissolved salts, and less heat than hoped for was extracted.

Steam | Cold water

Hot rocks

▼ Wave machines

Ocean waves store an enormous amount of energy, but extracting it is difficult. Tests done on wave machines show that they can make a contribution, but they have to be very solidly built to survive, which makes them expensive.

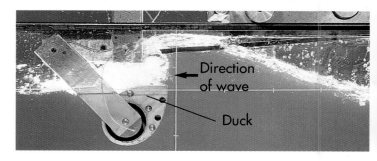

Waves coming from the right make the leading edge of a Salter's duck wave machine bob up and down. A device called a dynamo converts the motion into electricity.

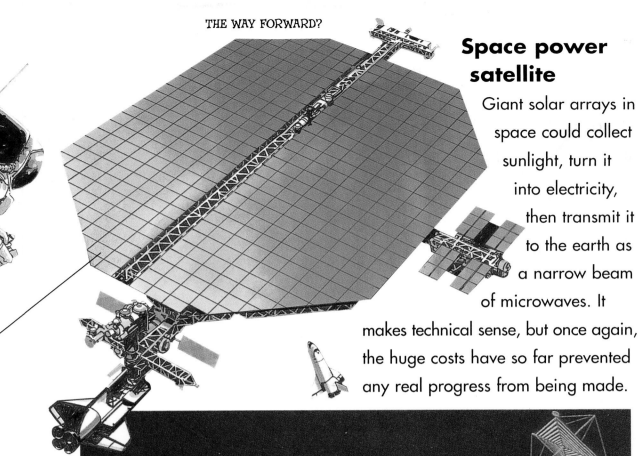

Solar array

Space power satellite

Giant solar arrays in space could collect sunlight, turn it into electricity, then transmit it to the earth as a narrow beam of microwaves. It makes technical sense, but once again, the huge costs have so far prevented any real progress from being made.

► Microwaves

The beam of microwaves transmitted from a solar space station (above) would be converted back into electricity using large collectors. The beam would need to be pointed accurately so the radiation did not stray and harm nearby plants or people.

TALKING POINT

All the new sources seem to have technical, financial, or practical problems.

Q: Does it make sense to work on far-out ideas? Shouldn't we find a single new source to replace fossil fuels?

A: There doesn't seem to be a single replacement source, so any sensible new source must be tried to see if it can contribute.

Look Back and Find

How much do you know about new energy sources? Here are some questions to test your knowledge. If you don't know an answer, you can find it somewhere in the book.

New energy sources

Coal, oil, and gas haven't run out yet, and probably won't for many decades. So why are so many people worrying about new sources of energy? What changes in the world are making the search for new sources so urgent?

The sun

It may be 93 million miles away, but the sun still controls our energy supplies. Can you name six kinds of energy that come from the sun, either directly or indirectly, including the sunshine of millions of years ago? And can you name two sources of energy that don't rely on the sun?

What is energy?

One of the most basic laws of science states that energy can neither be created nor destroyed. So what are we doing when we eat sugar, strike a match, or burn a log or a piece of coal? One moment it's there, and the next it's gone. Doesn't that mean that the energy has been destroyed?

Energy conservation

Saving energy makes sense. With careful use, we could make our energy sources last twice as long. So why don't we try harder? And why do so many well-meaning attempts to save energy — better light bulbs or more efficient engines, for example — achieve less than hoped?

Hydrogen

Many experts think that the fuel of the future is hydrogen — a light, odorless, colorless gas. Why do they think it would be so good, compared to, say, gasoline or diesel? Can you think of two different ways in which hydrogen could be used to drive a car?

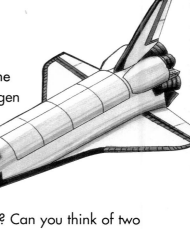

Solar energy

The sun is five billion years old and will go on shining for another five billion years. Does it produce enough energy to supply all our needs? If so, what is the problem? Describe two different ways of using solar energy.

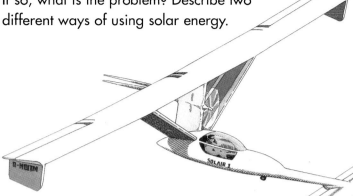

Wind and water

Wind power and water power are two ancient sources of energy that were rediscovered in the late twentieth century. Which is more important at the moment as a source of energy for the world? What about the future? What are the prospects, and the limitations, of wind and water power?

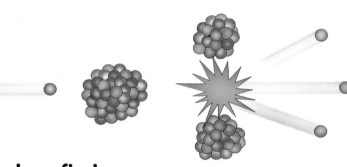

Biomass

Biomass is an unusual word, but what does it mean? When you collect firewood, what you are collecting is biomass. Name three other forms of biomass, and how they might be used by different people as a source of energy.

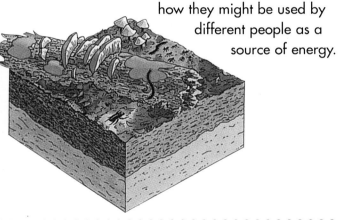

Nuclear fission

France lacks its own supplies of oil or gas, so it decided twenty years ago to build a large number of identical nuclear plants. Now almost all of France's electricity comes from these plants, which work well. Why haven't other countries done the same? Do you think they will in the future, and if not, why not?

Deciding priorities

In replacing fossil fuels, we have plenty of choices but none of them can do the job alone. Name some of the small-scale technologies that may ease problems locally. Which big technologies do you think deserve the most support?

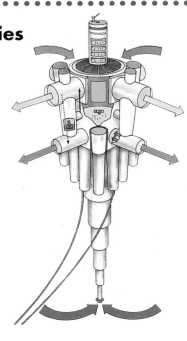

Global warming

Governments all over the world have agreed to cut carbon dioxide emissions by the year 2010, but at the moment the targets look like they won't be met by most countries. Why does it take so long for new energy sources to be adopted? If nuclear power is abandoned, is this likely to make things better or worse?

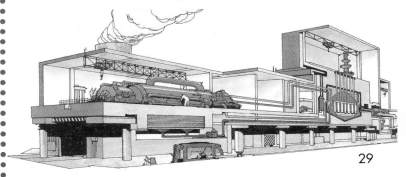

You Be Environmental!

Given the scale of the problem, it may seem that nothing you can do will have any effect on our energy sources. But this isn't true. If we all tried harder not to use energy wastefully, air pollution and global warming would be reduced. Turning off lights and heating when they aren't needed, insulating homes, and walking instead of taking the car on short trips make sense, save money, and could help save our world.

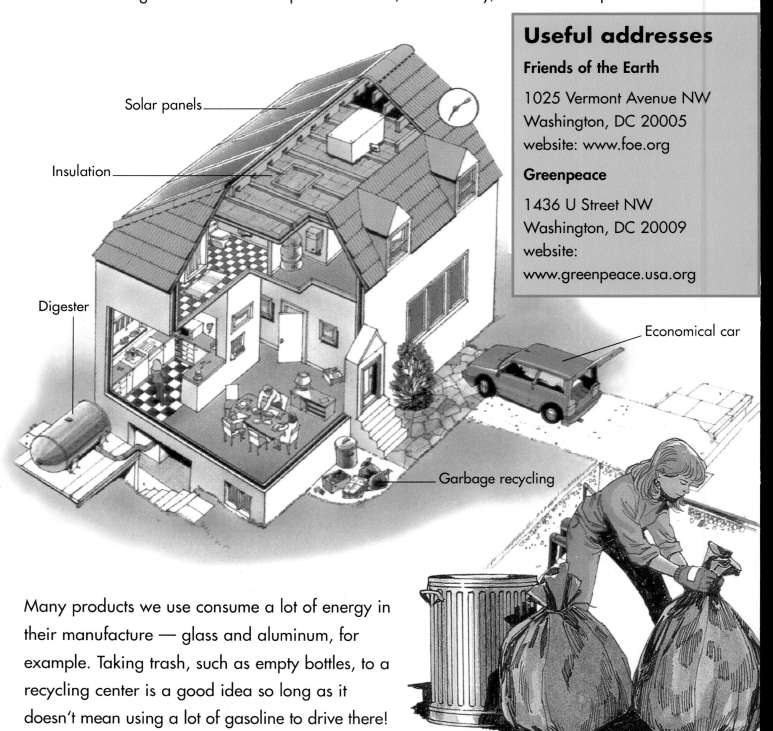

Solar panels

Insulation

Digester

Economical car

Garbage recycling

Useful addresses

Friends of the Earth

1025 Vermont Avenue NW
Washington, DC 20005
website: www.foe.org

Greenpeace

1436 U Street NW
Washington, DC 20009
website:
www.greenpeace.usa.org

Many products we use consume a lot of energy in their manufacture — glass and aluminum, for example. Taking trash, such as empty bottles, to a recycling center is a good idea so long as it doesn't mean using a lot of gasoline to drive there!

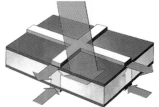

GLOSSARY

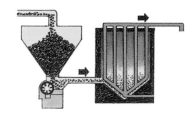

Biomass
The products of growing plants, which include leaves, timber, and alcohol from fermentation.

Electrolyte
The material in a battery that takes part in a chemical reaction to produce electricity.

Emissions
Fumes produced by burning fuel that are released into the environment through exhaust pipes and chimneys.

Fermentation
A chemical reaction in which the sugar in a plant is converted into alcohol.

Fission
The splitting of a heavy atom of uranium or plutonium to make lighter atoms and release a lot of energy. Used in nuclear power stations and atomic bombs.

Fluorescent
Describes something, such as a light bulb, that creates light by making chemicals glow.

Fossil fuels
Fuels such as coal, oil, and gas. They are formed from the preserved remains (fossils) of plants and animals that lived millions of years ago.

Fusion
The combination of two light atoms to make a heavier one, releasing energy. The source of the sun's power and hydrogen bombs.

Geothermal
Describes the heat of the earth, produced deep in the interior, which reaches the surface as hot springs and volcanoes.

Landfill sites
Holes in the ground, often left by quarrying, that are used as garbage dumps.

Megawatt
A measure of the power of an energy source, equal to one million watts, or one thousand kilowatts.

Methane
A gas, also known as natural gas, made up of one part carbon to four parts hydrogen.

Sustainable sources
Energy sources that can continue indefinitely, as they do not depend on a limited supply of fuel.

Turbine
A fan or propellerlike device, used in the generation of electricity, that turns a flow of water or air into rotary (circular) motion.

INDEX

A
alcohol 20, 31
atmosphere 5
atoms 22, 23, 24, 25, 31

B
batteries 10, 11, 31
biogas 21
biomass 20, 29, 31

C
carbon dioxide 5, 13, 22, 23, 29
catalyst 12
climate 5
clockwork radio 11
coal 4, 5, 7, 22, 28, 31
conservation 8, 9, 28
currents 10, 14

D
diesel 8, 23, 28

E
earth, the 5, 7, 12, 26, 27, 31

electric car 10, 11
electricity 10, 11, 12, 14, 15, 16, 17, 18, 19, 22, 23, 26, 27, 29, 31
electrolyte 10, 12, 31
emissions 13, 23, 31
engines 8, 11, 12, 13, 23

F
fermentation 20, 21, 31
fission 22, 23, 24, 25, 29, 31
fluorescent 9, 31
fossil fuels 7, 27, 29, 31
fuel 5, 6, 7, 8, 9, 12, 13, 16, 18, 20, 21, 22, 23, 25, 27, 31
fuel cells 12, 13
fusion 24, 25, 31

G
gas 4, 5, 7, 20, 21, 26, 28, 31
gasoline 8, 11, 13, 20, 28
geothermal 7, 26, 31
global warming 5, 8, 22, 23, 29, 30

H
helium 13, 24
hybrid car 11

hydroelectric projects 11, 16, 17
hydrogen 12, 13, 24, 25, 28, 31

L
landfill sites 20, 21, 31
light bulbs 9, 31

M
megawatt 16, 22, 31
methane 21, 31
microwaves 27

N
nuclear energy 7
nuclear fission *see fission*
nuclear fusion *see fusion*
nuclear power 22, 23, 29, 31

O
oil 4, 5, 7, 8, 28, 31
oxygen 6, 12

P
plutonium 22, 31
pollution 5, 8, 12, 15, 30
population 4, 20, 21
power stations 5, 10, 12, 14, 16, 22, 24, 26, 31

R
radiation 23, 24, 27
radioactivity 23
recycling 8, 9, 30

S
solar energy 6, 7, 29
solar panels 14, 27, 3
solar power 5, 14, 15, 2
space 12, 27
sun, the 4, 5, 6, 7, 14, 1 17, 22, 24, 28, 29, 31
sustainable sources 5, 3

T
tidal energy 7
tidal power 1
turbine 16, 17, 18, 19, 22, 26, 31

U
uranium 22, 23, 31

W
water power 11, 16, 17 25, 29
wave machines 26
windmills 18, 19
wind power 18, 19, 25, 2
wood 6, 9, 20, 21, 29

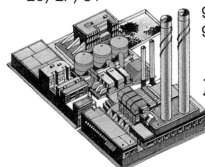

Picture Credits

Abbreviations: t-top, m-middle, b-bottom, r-right, l-left.

Cover & pages 8b, 18t & 26m - Solution Pictures. 4, 10 both, 12, 13t, 16, 17m, 22 & 23t - Rex Features. 5, 11t, 13b, 20m, 23b & 25 - Frank Spooner Pictures. 6b, 14, 15 both & 20b - Eye Ubiquitous. 7, 9br & 26b - James Davis Travel Photography. 8-9m - BMW. 9ml - Paul Nightingale. 17t - Oxford Scientific Films. 18m & 21 - Science Photo Library.